#15#

D1403181

I LIKE MIXED-BREED DOGS!

Linda Bozzo

DISCOVER DOGS WITH THE AMERICAN CANINE ASSOCIATION

ICA, a subdivision of ACA

INTERNATIONAL CANINE ASSOCIATION INC.
ICA
OFFICIAL SEAL
"Tracking your pets around the world"

ICA, a subdivision of ACA

It is the Mission of the American Canine Association (ACA), and its subdivision, the International Canine Association (ICA), to provide registered dog owners with the educational support needed for raising, training, showing, and breeding the healthiest pets expected by responsible pet owners throughout the world. Through our activities and services, we encourage and support the dog world in order to promote best-known husbandry standards as well as to ensure that the voice and needs of our customers are quickly and properly addressed.

Our continued support, commitment, and direction are guided by our customers, including veterinary, legal, and legislative advisors. ACA aims to provide the most efficient, cooperative, and courteous service to our customers and strives to set the standard for education and problem solving for all who depend on our services.

For more information, please visit www.acacanines.com, e-mail customerservice@acadogs.com, phone 1-800-651-8332, or write to the American Canine Association at PO Box 121107, Clermont, FL 34712.

Enslow Elementary, an imprint of Enslow Publishers, Inc.

Enslow Elementary® is a registered trademark of Enslow Publishers, Inc.

Copyright © 2012 by Enslow Publishers, Inc.

Library of Congress Cataloging-in-Publication Data

Bozzo, Linda.

I like mixed-breed dogs! / Linda Bozzo.

  p. cm. — (Discover dogs with the American Canine Association)

Includes bibliographical references and index.

Summary: "Early readers will learn how to care for a mixed-breed dog"—Provided by publisher.

ISBN 978-0-7660-3845-5

1. Mutts (Dogs)—Juvenile literature. I. Title.

SF427.B687 2012

636.7—dc22

2011010472

Future editions:

Paperback ISBN 978-1-4644-0122-0

ePUB ISBN 978-1-4645-1029-8

PDF ISBN 978-1-4646-1029-5

Printed in China

012012 Leo Paper Group, Heshan City, Guangdong, China

10 9 8 7 6 5 4 3 2 1

To Our Readers: We have done our best to make sure all Internet Addresses in this book were active and appropriate when we went to press. However, the author and the publisher have no control over and assume no liability for the material available on those Internet sites or on other Web sites they may link to. Any comments or suggestions can be sent by e-mail to comments@enslow.com or to the address on the back cover.

Every effort has been made to locate all copyright holders of material used in this book. If any errors or omissions have occurred, corrections will be made in future editions of this book.

Photo Credits: Angelika Fischer/Photos.com, p. 13 (hamburger); Annette Shaff/Photos.com, p. 13 (collar); Catherine Yeulet/Photos.com, p. 17; Claudia Närdemann/Photos.com, p. 1; Comstock Images/Photos.com, pp. 8, 18; Grant Shimmin/Photos.com, p. 13; jclegg/Photos.com, p. 13 (leash and rope); Joyce Marrero/Photos.com, p. 11; Jupiterimages/Photos.com, p. 3 (left); Novosti/Photo Researchers, Inc., p. 19; Rebecca Barr/Photos.com, p. 3 (right); Shutterstock.com, pp. 5, 6, 10, 13 (bed, bowls, brush), 14, 21, 23; Stefan Petru Andronache/Photos.com, p. 7; Zhang Bo/Photos.com, p. 9.

Cover Photo: Shutterstock.com (beige puppy with a red collar).

Enslow Elementary

an imprint of

Enslow Publishers, Inc.

40 Industrial Road
Box 398
Berkeley Heights, NJ 07922
USA

http://www.enslow.com

CONTENTS

IS A MIXED-BREED DOG RIGHT FOR YOU?

A breed is a type of dog. Mixed-breed dogs are more than one breed. They come in many different sizes and colors.

Many mixed-breed dogs can be found at animal shelters. They do not usually cost much. Each dog is different. Choose a gentle dog that is good with children.

Mixed-breed dogs in shelters are waiting for someone to take them home.

Puppies are full of energy! Can your family keep up?

A DOG OR PUPPY?

Puppies are fun, but training one takes time. They also need a lot of attention. An older dog may already be trained and be easier to care for. Which would be better for your family?

LOVING YOUR MIXED-BREED DOG

All dogs need love. Pet your dog and talk to him. Spend time with him, and he will love you back.

Dogs have much
love to share!

Teach your dog
to play fetch!

EXERCISE

Walk your dog every day using a **leash**. Playing games, like **fetch**, with your dog is good exercise too.

Running keeps him healthy.

FEEDING YOUR MIXED-BREED DOG

Dogs can be fed wet or dry dog food. Ask a veterinarian (vet), a doctor for animals, which food to feed your dog and how much to feed her. Give your mixed-breed dog fresh, clean water every day.

Remember to keep your dog's food and water dishes clean. Dirty dishes can make her sick.

Do not feed your mixed-breed dog people food. It can make her sick.

Your new dog will need:

a collar with a tag

a bed

a brush

food and water dishes

a leash

toys

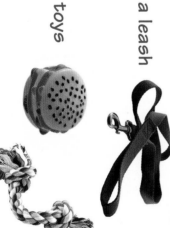

Some dogs love water. Others might try to get away.

GROOMING

Most dogs need to be brushed once a week. Dogs with longer hair may need to be brushed more often.

Give your dog a bath with gentle soap made just for dogs. How often you bathe your dog depends on your dog's breeds.

You also need to clip your dog's nails. A vet or **groomer** can show you how.

WHAT YOU SHOULD KNOW

It can be hard to figure out any health problems if you do not know the breeds of your dog. Your vet can do a test that can help find out your dog's breeds.

The breeds of your dog will give you an idea how long your dog might live. Generally, smaller dogs live longer than larger dogs.

Your dog will love
you for as long
as he lives.

You will need to take your new dog to the vet for a checkup. He will need shots, called vaccinations, and yearly checkups to keep him healthy. If you think your dog may be sick or hurt, call your vet.

A GOOD FRIEND

With good care and lots of love, your mixed-breed dog will be a good friend to you for many years.

FUN FACT:

Strelka (black and white) and Belka (white) were both mixed-breed dogs that went into space. They returned to Earth safely.

NOTE TO PARENTS

It is important to consider having your dog spayed or neutered when the dog is young. Spaying and neutering are operations that prevent unwanted puppies and can help improve the overall health of your dog.

It is also a good idea to microchip your dog, in case he or she gets lost. A vet will implant a microchip under the skin that contains your contact information, which can then be scanned at a vet's office or animal shelter.

Some towns require licenses for dogs, so be sure to check with your town clerk.

For more information, speak with a vet.

Make sure you have everything your new dog will need before you bring her home.

Words to Know

animal shelter—A place where dogs who do not have homes stay.

breed—A type of dog.

fetch—To go after a toy and bring it back.

groomer—A person who cuts a dog's fur and nails.

leash—A chain or strap that connects to a dog's collar.

vaccination—A shot that dogs need to stay healthy.

veterinarian (vet)—A doctor for animals.

Books

Ganeri, Anita. *Dogs*. Chicago, Ill.: Heinemann
Library, 2009.

Paley, Rebecca. *Dogs 101*. New York: Scholastic, Inc.,
2010.

Internet Addresses

American Canine Association: Kids Corner
<http://acakids.com/>

**Janet Wall's How to Love Your Dog:
Mixed Breeds**
<http://loveyourdog.com/mixedbreeds.html>

INDEX

A
animal shelter, 4, 20
attention, 7

B
bathing, 15
bed, 13
Belka, 19
brush, 13

C
checkup, 18
clipping (nails), 15
collar, 13
cost, 4

E
exercise, 11

F
fetch, 11
food, 12
   dish, 12, 13

G
games, 11
grooming, 15

L
leash, 11, 13
license, 20

M
microchip, 20

N
neutering, 20

P
playing, 11
puppies, 7, 20

S
spaying, 20
Strelka, 19

T
tag, 13
toys, 13
training, 7

V
vaccinations, 18
veterinarian (vet), 12, 15,
   18, 20

W
walking, 11
water, 12
   dish, 12, 13